Tips on N...
Your S...

it Girl Rules
IT'S GETTING HAUTE IN HERE

TAMIKA NURSE

The It Girl Rules
Copyright © 2010 by Tamika Nurse
ISBN-13: 978-0-9832539-0-7
Library of Congress Control Number: 2011900420

First Edition

All rights reserved. No part of this book may be used, reproduced, stored, or transmitted in any manner whatsoever — whether auditory, graphic, mechanical, or electronic, including photocopying – without written permission, except in the case of brief excerpts used in critical articles and reviews. Unauthorized reproduction of any part of this work is illegal and is punishable by law.

The purpose of this book is to encourage the reader. The publisher and the author shall have neither liability nor responsibility to any person or entity with respect to any loss or damage, caused or alleged to be caused, directly or indirectly by the information contained in this book.

Book Design: DLGD LLC

It Girl Industries
www.itgirlrules.com
info@itgirlrules.com

To my beautiful mother, with love.

CONTENTS

Introduction **6**

I. WEAR IT
Fashion fundamentals **13**

Fit **15**
Underwear **17**
Tailoring **20**
Tailoring Don'ts **23**
Fabrics **25**
Color **28**
Additional Tips and Tricks **30**

II. STYLE IT
Defining your personal style **33**

Signature Style **35**
Style @ Work **37**
Faux Style/Knock-offs **39**

III. SHOP IT
Shopping ABCs —
How, Where, and When to shop **43**

Pre-shopping Closet Purge **45**
The Shopping Experience **48**
Shop and Save **51**
The Fitting Room **60**
Returns **63**
Power Shopping **67**

....

The *It Girl Rules* Rewound 74

INTRODUCTION

The *It Girl Rules* series is simply a culmination of my inner-dialog, my musings, my insights and my philosophies on style, career, and personal growth. This is my formal reply to every woman who has ever asked for my advice or opinion on these topics. You were my original inspiration for this project.

For women who were on the road to self-improvement and somehow got off-course or simply recognize the need for a change, please think of this book as a catalyst, a kick out of your comfort zone and an outright challenge to complacency. My goal is to stir up your creativity and your motivation to do what is necessary to become your best self.

Who is the *It Girl*? In my opinion, she is the inspirational superwoman that we are all striving to become.

The *It Girl* has enough "diva-tude" to command all eyes in a room, but possesses the grace and humility to be approachable and inviting. She understands that her external beauty truly comes from the inside. Beyond the accoutrements and beyond the glamour, we are all human beings. The *It Girl* is grounded in that.

The *It Girl* is self aware, knowing what her strengths and weaknesses are. She recognizes that her road to self-improvement has no true end. Despite life's ups and downs, her goal is to live a full life and to enjoy every day.

The *It Girl* also understands the importance of connecting with people. She has a generous spirit, with the ability to show love and receive love. The *It Girl* is not selfish. No. She is a giving person — whether it means giving of her energy, time, or finances to her family, friends or causes that are important to her.

The *It Girl* respects others. She believes that every person has value and respects their differences. She comfortably maneuvers among royalty and those who live in poverty. She shows the same consideration to the janitor and the CEO.

The *It Girl* respects herself. She does not accept ill-treatment or disrespect of any kind from anyone. With humility and strength, she embraces and celebrates her self-worth. She knows that she is a queen and should be treated as such.

The *It Girl* does not live her life by convenience or preference; she lives by convictions and values.

I digress.

In Volume I of this series, my focus is on style and fashion — topics near and dear to my heart. To all my fellow *It Girls*-in-training, I hope you enjoy reading this as much I have enjoyed writing it.

No more talking about IT, now is the time to be about IT!

Jamika

*Tips on Navigating
Your Style Journey*

THE it Girl Rules
IT'S GETTING HAUTE IN HER

*All I want are high heels, high heels.
If I was a girl, I'd wear a lot of high heels.
High, stiletto heels.*

Isaac Mizrahi

I. Wear It
FASHION FUNDAMENTALS

On this style journey, It Girls have to be prepared with a little bit of patience and a sense of humor.

You should also love the body that you have today — knowing that your body is beautiful and unique. Each of us reflects God's masterful creation. He loves everything about you, so you should love all of you too. If your goal is to make changes to your body before embarking on this journey, then that's a personal decision. However, I advocate dressing the person you are today. Whenever you do achieve your physical or weight goals, then dress your new body at that time. In the meantime, enhance your look in a creative way by wearing garments that fit your body type.

It's a marathon and not a sprint. So give yourself permission to invest time to figure out what works and what does not work. And most of all enjoy the journey.

FIT

Fit accounts for over 50% of the success of any look, in my opinion. If your clothes fit properly — not too short, not too long, not too loose, and not too tight, then you automatically look good. Great fitting clothes do not have to be expensive either. You can wear the most famous high-end couture label and still appear to be unkempt because it doesn't fit you properly. Last, but not least, you do not need to be a size 4 to find clothing that fits. The key to buying clothing off-the-rack is to find labels with a balance of the style you desire and a fit that complements your body type.

Please keep in mind that every designer uses different fit models to determine their sizing charts and the cut of their garments. A fit model is a person or mannequin that represents a specific size, like the size medium or the size 16. Then, designers will pattern their garments against those models. Fit models vary dramatically across designers. This is the reason why sizing and tailoring are so different across brands. For example, you may be able to fit a Small perfectly in one brand, but find that

Medium fits better in a different brand. *It Girls* understand these nuances and are prepared to professionally tailor their clothing since it's very rare for any woman to consistently find a perfect fit.

UNDERWEAR

As we discussed earlier, you will look exponentially better when a garment fits properly — this includes both outer garments and undergarments. That's why *It Girls* invest in underwear that fits perfectly, because it literally lays the foundation for the successful fit of any outerwear.

Did you know that most women do not wear the proper size bra? Some statistics state that up to 85 percent of women are wearing the wrong bra size. It is easy to get stuck in a certain size. However, our breasts will change due to puberty, pregnancy, changes in weight, etc. If you are currently spilling out on top, on the sides, or underneath, then it's definitely time to change your bra size. There is also a risk to your health, in terms of back pain and poor posture.

Some women are very uncomfortable with G-strings or thongs. I say 'get really comfortable with them' because panty lines are grounds for arrest. Panty lines (the seams of your panties) should never be seen through pants, dresses, skirts, shorts, or jeans — ever, ever, never, never! Panty lines are just a HUGE

NO-NO!! Full panties are not a problem as long as no one can see the lines. Many intimate apparel designers have introduced "seamless" panties. I still do not totally trust them, but they are worth a try. You have to use your judgment. When you check out your outfit in the mirror, do not only look at the front. Please use a second mirror and look at the back too! Standing with your back to the mirror and turning your neck to get a glimpse will not give you a complete view. Make sure you know exactly what's going on 'back there' before you leave home.

Another great foundational garment is Spanx, which offers many shapewear options for tummy control and bottom shaping. It may even reduce your dress size because it smoothes you out so much. Spanx are very comfortable as long as you find the right size. For someone who is normally a size Medium, the Large Spanx could be more comfortable because of the natural compression that occurs. If you purchase the wrong size, then it will feel uncomfortable, ride up, and may cut off your circulation.

There are many great brands that offer a variety of awesome, quality foundational garments like Victoria's Secret. Don't overlook Nordstrom, Bloomingdales, and Saks Fifth Avenue. Usually the upscale retailers sell high quality underwear from the best designers and offer the widest variety of sizes.

TAILORING

For the *It Girl* that cannot find brands that fit 'just right' or wants to improve the fit of an existing garment, then tailoring is the best option. You will save some time and money by selecting clothing that needs minimal alterations. Shop for garments that fit the widest part of you and the tailor will do the rest. For example, I would advise bustier sisters to find button down shirts that fit your bust comfortably and then ask your tailor to take in the seams underneath your bust line. Not only will the shirt be tailor made for you, but it will also appear more luxe. This rule also applies to curvy women that rarely find jeans or pants that fit because of their waist-to-hips ratio. Tailoring is the solution for that menacing 'gap' at your waist. After you find slacks that fit your hips and thighs, then ask your tailor to add darts to the waist. It's that simple.

For the very short or very tall *It Girl*, online shopping provides an infinite world of special sizing options outside of the limited in-store selection. There are far less items available for taller women, but retailers like Victoria's

Secret, Top Shop and Banana Republic have dedicated 'Tall' departments within their online stores. In addition, height-conscious shops like Tall Girl are in many major markets and have an online store as well. However, a tailor can always shorten or lengthen the sleeves or hems of regular-sized clothing. Lengthening can be tricky, so make sure that the hem or sleeve of your garment has enough extra material for the tailor to work with.

It Girls choose professionals to make sure their tailoring is done right. Many mid-tier and high-end retailers have professional tailors staffed within their shops, including Bloomingdales, Nordstrom, and Burlington Coat Factory. They will tailor virtually any garment purchased inside or outside of their stores. Although alterations services at these types of retailers are not cheap, significant discounts or even free alterations are available for garments purchased at their respective stores.

Tailoring on-the-cheap or without a reference is risky because your garments may be destroyed or may not be altered correctly. Ask for referrals instead. Also, many large malls with high-end anchor stores, like Saks Fifth Avenue or Neiman Marcus, will have at least one independently owned tailor on the premises. There is some inherent credibility since these establishments specialize in tailoring and are connected with the mall. They also tend to be much less expensive than the tailors within the department stores. However, I advise that you alter something easy first before giving them a more difficult tailoring job. Lastly, stay away from your local dry cleaners for alterations unless the job is very simple, like replacing a button or fixing a hem. If your dry cleaner does not have a professional seamstress or tailor on staff, then beware.

TAILORING DON'TS

It Girls limit their use of safety pins to hold fabrics together or to create a dart. If the safety pin opens up accidently, then you will probably get pricked. Not only will that hurt, but you may even bleed. That is not how *It Girls* roll. When you have to use these apparatuses to make your garment fit, then it's a good indicator that it needs to be permanently fixed, tailored, tossed, or donated.

There are always exceptions. If you inadvertently lose a shirt button, then you will need a safety pin to hold your shirt together. Sometimes a pants zipper will split or get stuck and a safety pin (or two) will hold everything together until you can actually change clothes. Safety pins also come in handy when you are surprised that a particular garment does not fit the way it once did, but you 'have to' wear it for some reason. It's life and mishaps will occur to all of us at some point. As a matter of fact, I keep a safety pin in my makeup case at all times — just in case.

Belts become a "don't" when they are used to replace proper tailoring. Similar to the safety pins scenario, belts should not be used to force your pants to fit or to keep your pants from falling down. Pants or jeans should fit properly without your belt. However, it is a fashion accessory that is used for practical purposes. For example, if you have a shirt tucked into a pair of pants, then the belt neatly pulls the look together — literally and figuratively.

While an *It Girl* will not wear clothing that does not fit properly as a general rule, creativity is sometimes needed to make a garment work when it's not 'acting right.' However, these fixes should be viewed as temporary solutions only and not a substitute for professional alterations.

FABRICS

Garments made of synthetic fabrics like polyester and acrylic are usually inexpensive, but don't have the longevity or quality of their natural counterparts. In other words, you will often find these textiles in the 'disposable clothing' that you wear for one or two seasons and then toss. Polyester is not a bad fabric, but it can look cheap depending on the quality of the material and the fabric care used. For example, polyester may not hold up to multiple ironings because it tends to get shiny. Almost all acrylics will fade, lose shape, and get fuzzy after being worn a few times and after a handful of cleanings. If you must purchase acrylic or polyester, then choose garments that are blended with cotton or wool. Lycra is synthetic as well. However, I'm a big fan of Lycra, like most women. My advice is to stay under 4% or your garment may not snap back after it is stretched out.

Natural fabrics like cotton, wool, silk, or linen are best, because these materials usually look better and last longer. Fabric care can add up for wools, silks and linens, because of the cost of dry cleaning. Conversely, most cotton is machine washable. The down side is that colors can fade and fabrics can be damaged in the washing machine if the wrong temperature, detergent, or wash cycle is chosen. Silks are found in some of the most beautiful feminine garments, like blouses and dresses. However, it's a delicate material that doesn't like perspiration of any kind. The moisture will leave an indelible mark when it dries that can only be removed by a dry cleaner. Linen is also a beautiful, breathable fabric. It feels good on the skin, especially in warm weather. However, linen is notorious for wrinkles — no matter how much you iron. Linen is also a bit see-through. For women who wear a linen skirt, dress, or pants, you have to determine how comfortable you are with the transparency of the material. Consider choosing a heavier grade of linen, linen with complementary lining, or linen blended with cotton to decrease transparency and the appearance of wrinkles.

Leather generally has more longevity than its less expensive, synthetic counterpart; i.e. artificial leather or pleather. Quality leather shoes, handbags, or coats are an investment that could last a lifetime, with the proper maintenance. To the untrained eye, it is actually very difficult to tell the difference between certain leather and pleather designs. However, pleather garments and accessories do not last as long because they cannot withstand the same amount of wear and tear as leather.

COLOR

Neutrals like black, brown, beige, or white are 'safe' colors because they can be worn with almost anything you own. Black is probably the safest color choice. 99% of the population cannot go wrong with the color black, but you don't have to stay there. Colors are fun. Find the ones that work best for you. How? You may have to do some research. I recommend that you look at several fashion magazines and pay close attention to the women with skin tones that are close to your own. You will begin to notice that a consistent color palette is being used. This is a good indication that those same colors will work for you also. Research doesn't trump practical application. So please be prepared for a little trial and error as well.

There is no need to completely revamp your wardrobe. I recommend that you start with a few key accessories that will give you a pop of color; jewelry, belts, scarves, hosiery, handbags or shoes, that complement the neutral colors in your existing wardrobe. Here is your chance to experiment with a new bold color, like red, orange, pink, green, or yellow, while curtailing costs. When you're ready, the next step is to incorporate more accent colors into your wardrobe — maybe start with a blouse. Please keep in mind that I'm not suggesting a Skittles approach to style here. However, one or two accent colors with a neutral outfit will add depth and dimension to your style that will be admired and make you stand out.

ADDITIONAL TIPS AND TRICKS

The local shoe repair shop is a great resource for non-shoe repairs. They will fix or replace straps and zippers on handbags that may be ripped or broken. If you have a belt that is too tight or not tight enough, they can actually add holes that are the right size and symmetrically spaced. Gone are the days that you use a nail or knife or God-knows-what to add holes to your belt.

For the *It Girl* who is extremely tight on time and/or is not adept at ironing, your local dry cleaners can help. For just a few dollars, they will press your pre-washed shirts or pants. However, you must specifically request "Press Only" or you will have sticker shock when you see your next dry cleaning bill. Please note that some fabrics cannot handle the agitation of a washing machine, even when the fabric care instructions state "machine washable." For hand washable garments, dry cleaning is best as there is a risk of shrinking, discoloration, or destroying the garment.

Lint on clothing can be really annoying, especially for those who wear a lot of black. To remove lint in lieu of a lint brush or roller, you can always use packing tape or masking tape. If you are totally stuck, then use regular invisible tape. It's not as efficient, but it will get the job done. To avoid lint, always ask for a black cloth napkin when dining at a restaurant. Some may not have it, but it never hurts to ask.

Consider investing in a garment steamer. They are great for removing pesky wrinkles without ironing. These steamers are incredibly user-friendly and work fast. For about $40, you can purchase a decent steamer. Like ironing, there is a risk of being burned with improper use so please read through all the instructions first. If you travel often for business, then perhaps a portable personal steamer is right for you.

A girl should be two things: classy and fabulous.

Coco Chanel

Classic style is the cornerstone of fashion. We all have those timeless garments and accessories that can be dusted off five or ten years from now and still be worn with confidence. Classic clothing is an investment that will pay dividends, because you will not have to spend money every season to keep up with changing trends. A good example of a classic is the little black dress or a tailored black suit. These never go out of style. Jacqueline Onassis, Grace Kelly and Audrey Hepburn are not only famous because of their public life in film, entertainment and politics. These fierce women were also fashion icons in the 1940's, 1950's and 1960's who embodied classic, yet contemporary style — most of which could easily be worn today.

Once you understand what your classics are, then you should feel free to experiment with trends or fads. What is a fad? A good litmus test is to ask yourself, "If no one else wore this, would I still wear it?" If the answer is no, then you have stumbled onto a fad. Footless tights and leg warmers are definitely examples of fads or trendy clothing. I'm not knocking trends, because I absolutely believe that they are necessary to push the boundaries and keep fashion moving forward. However, it is important to understand the difference between classics and fads and have a good balance of both in your wardrobe.

SIGNATURE STYLE

If you observe celebrities, you quickly recognize that many have a signature style. A celebrity's signature becomes forever tied to their persona and people want to copy it. Madonna's signature style in the late 1980's was so impactful to the world of fashion that she will forever be associated with funky lace outfits accompanied by fishnets and capris. Young girls copied her then and they are still copying her style now.

Maybe there is a style that you have wanted to experiment with for a while. It's okay to try new things. Go for it, get comfortable with it, and own it. You probably already have a signature and do not even know it. Fill in the blank in the following statement: If I left the house without wearing my "_____," then I would not feel like I am fully dressed (underwear, not withstanding). My answer is a right-hand ring. Your answer might be oversized sunglasses, a locket, a blazer, a scarf, bright nail polish, or a vintage handbag. Whatever style statement you choose, put your personal signature on it and embrace it. Make it synonymous with who you are, because it's yours. However, you are free to change it any time.

So what is your style statement going to be? Sometimes, it helps to put your ideas on paper. Consider a vision map. Vision mapping will bring your fashion-related inspirations and observations to life. It's simple. All you have to do is clip images and phrases out of magazines (that you own) and assemble them into a collage on poster board or something similar. There is no wrong way to do it. As long as it reflects your personal goals, then it's perfect. Once you're done, display your map prominently as a daily reminder of those goals — maybe in your bathroom.

STYLE @ WORK

It Girls know that fashion plays a key role in perceived professionalism at the work place. No, it is not fair but it is true. If you are not where you want to be professionally, you can still dress like you are already in that position. For example, if your goal is to work in senior management or even become the CEO, then why not dress the part today? In other words, "Fake it until you make it." The very act of dressing-the-part creates an incredibly empowering mindset and will eventually impact your demeanor. You never know when you'll be called into a senior executive's office for a meeting or presentation — by surprise or on purpose. Either way, your goal is to be prepared for anything.

Furthermore, *It Girls* want respect and career advancement based on skills, accomplishments and results — not because of other "assets." A fashion statement laced with sexual innuendo — either too tight or too revealing — is inappropriate and a distraction in a corporate setting. Cleavage, painted on jeans or pants, extremely short skirts, and halter tops are definitely cause for concern and will get you noticed in the workplace for all the wrong reasons. Breaking through the glass ceiling has been tough enough for women; fashion should not further impede our progress.

This does not mean that you are supposed to wear a suit every day since most companies observe a business casual dress code. However, your work wardrobe should consist of complementary staples, like blouses, camisoles, button down shirts, blazers, flat front pants, lined skirts, a few simple heels and reliable flats — all in your color palette. In extremely laid back work environments, polos, khaki pants and jeans may be more appropriate. Either way, please use your best judgment and do what works for your situation.

FAUX STYLE/KNOCK-OFFS

A knockoff is simply a copy or imitation. There are three tiers of knockoffs — (1) a counterfeit that illegally uses another designer's protected trademark, (2) a copycat design that does not use the original trademark, and (3) a design that is inspired by the original — not a copycat, but looks similar, and does not use the original trademark.

I'm from New York City and have spent a fair amount of time shopping in Chinatown. On Canal Street near Broadway, many street vendors and boutiques sell designer-labeled handbags, purses, sunglasses, shoes, and jewelry for a fraction of the original price. Despite the well-placed designer logos or trademarks (Louis Vuitton, Prada, Gucci or D&G), many people know that most of the merchandise is not authentic. Buying imitation merchandise is not illegal, but selling it is. It's a federal crime called "trafficking in counterfeit goods." There is a lot of police activity in Chinatown and similar markets throughout the country for this reason.

It's not my place to point a finger at anyone who chooses to buy knockoffs; especially the copycat or the inspired-by merchandise. However, you do not want to be in a situation where you are knowingly supporting illegal activity. It's more than a moral issue. You can actually be arrested and end up in jail.

Another danger of knockoffs is that you may be 'outed' by women who buy authentic merchandise and stay current on fashion trends. Someone with a very discerning eye can tell immediately that your knockoff is not real. God forbid that someone says to you, "I didn't see that at the Gucci store when I was shopping for my handbag." It's cheesy, but it could happen. And who wants to get 'called out' like that?

Visible designer labels are a bit overrated anyway. Louis Vuitton, Coach, Fendi and Gucci are notorious for producing designs with C's, F's, LVs, or G's all over the place. Every woman who purchases and wears their merchandise is essentially financing free advertising for that particular brand or designer. The only person that an *It Girl* is trying to advertise or showcase is herself. Fierce designs with understated labels and logos are ideal, in my opinion.

I shop, therefore I am.

Tammy Faye Bakker

III. Shop It

Shopping ABCs — How, Where, and When to Shop

Believe it or not, there is an It Girl sect out there that does not have the patience or the motivation to shop. (I hear the rest of you gasping and clutching your pearls! I'm doing the same thing!) For this special group of women who do not have the wherewithal to shop at the mall, at boutiques, or online, then the only substitute would be to get someone to do it for you: a personal shopper. Most high-end department stores and boutiques offer this fee-based service.

However, there is another group of women who are simply frustrated with the shopping process for a variety of other reasons. Don't give up, because there is hope and I'm here to help. I promise you that there are affordable brands and designers that will work really well for your particular body type, but it can take a while to figure out who they are. To shop successfully, all you need is some patience, along with a minimal investment of time and money.

PRE-SHOPPING CLOSET PURGE

Before you start shopping, audit your closet first. Your closet should be streamlined and only consist of the best: the bangers (translation: the unbelievably awesome), the winners, the garments and accessories that you are confident in and will wear at a moment's notice. Why keep something in your closet that you do not or will not wear? That precious real estate could be used for outfits that make you look amazing. If you haven't worn a garment or accessory in 18 to 24 months, then it's time to let it go — either give it away to someone who can use it or donate it to Goodwill. There are always exceptions, like clothing that is seasonal, for maternity, or only worn for very special occasions.

Redundancy is another issue. Do you naturally gravitate towards the same type of clothing or the same colors every time you shop? How many identical black skirts, khaki pants, blue jeans, or white shirts do you have in your closet? It's time to check yourself and to be honest about your shopping habits. My father's solution to curtailing clutter is to replace or discard something old each time he purchases something new. For example, if you decide to buy a pair of black shoes then you should concurrently get rid of the old pair of black shoes that have worn out. If you follow this philosophy, then you will have a well-balanced closet with virtually no redundancy or clutter.

In life, the very act of letting go can be difficult. However, it's the only way to make room for your blessings. In this context, the goal is to make room in your closet for the garments that look great on you and will enhance your wardrobe. If that criterion is not met, then you'll have to make the hard decision to let go of that garment or decide not to purchase it in the first place.

True commitment requires action. Please make a pact with yourself today to purge your closet within the next seven days and set a date on your calendar to complete this task. On average, you will only need two uninterrupted hours to completely purge your closet. In extreme cases when you have an abundance of clothing and multiple closets, then please budget four or more hours. To be most efficient with your time, focus on one thing at a time.

For example, start with shelves first followed by the left side of your closet and then the right side. Another approach is to clear out your closet by category — start with shoes, then coats, then dresses, and so on. Either way, consider keeping several large garbage bags handy to store everything that you are eliminating from your closet. If you choose to donate your clothing to charity, want a tax write-off, and do not have receipts, then prepare a written or typed list for your tax accountant with the approximate purchase price and the current fair market value of each item.

After your closet is purged, you can better identify the gaps in your wardrobe and then create your shopping list to fill those gaps. The next steps are to develop a reasonable budget and a timeline. There's no need to tackle the entire list in one shopping trip. It's okay to pace yourself. This is your personal journey and no one else's. Remember, it's a marathon, not a sprint. With your list, budget, timeline, and vision in place, you will be prepared to shop with confidence.

THE SHOPPING EXPERIENCE

What type of shopping experience do you enjoy most? Would you rather be left alone to figure things out? Or do you want some help every now and then as you shop? Your answers to these questions will help you to hone in on the retailers that are the best fit for your personality and your shopping needs.

Boutique shopping is usually more manageable than department stores. With smaller selections to navigate, you can shop with some level of confidence in a short amount of time and not feel overwhelmed by massive amounts of clothing choices. Department stores that are set up by designer or by brand will be simple for some and complex for others. Essentially, you will have to shop in each designer's area to find tops, jeans, accessories, jackets, suits or other items that fit. Unless you are intimately involved with a particular brand, then it becomes redundant and can be tiring. However, there are *It Girls* among us that love the hunt and never get tired. Some department stores also have garment specific sections dedicated to suits, dresses, coats, etc., which is great if you are looking for something very specific. For the window shopper that is just looking for ideas, then the retailer you choose does not matter as much.

There are pros and cons to both commissioned and non-commissioned sales environments. Commissioned sales associates receive a certain percentage of each sale that they make.

Discounters and mass merchandisers, like T.J.Maxx, Loehmann's or Target, do not normally have commissioned associates. Customer service at these establishments is decent, but minimal. The sales associates provide assistance when requested and will not pressure you to make a purchase. Traditional department stores like Lord & Taylor or Macy's fall in the middle. They will leave you alone, but the associates will occasionally ask if you need help. For the cashier that processes your sale, he or she will probably receive a nominal commission. The more upscale department stores like Nordstrom or Saks Fifth Avenue tend to have a more aggressive commissioned structure. The level of customer service is relatively high, but the associates will pressure you a bit to make that sale. A good way to gage which environment you are in is when a sales associate introduces themselves to you by their first name followed by, "If you need any assistance, please let me know." When you have made your final selections and are about to complete your purchase, the cashier will ask, "Who helped you today?" The associate who helped you will get acknowledged for closing the sale and will receive a commission or some type of incentive.

SHOP AND SAVE

It Girls do not have to pay full price for amazing clothing, accessories, shoes, or even makeup, unless she wants to. If you've got to have 'it' because you are working against a hard deadline, stuck with few options, or faced with an impossible circumstance — like attending a wedding in two days and you still haven't found a dress to wear, or you experience a sudden and unexpected cold snap while on vacation in the Caribbean and you didn't pack any warm clothing, then you may have to pay full price. These things happen. In all other circumstances, you are fully empowered to save money every time you shop.

DISCOUNTERS & CLOTHING OUTLETS

For those of you who are really patient, discount stores are a great way to save while you shop. I personally love Loehmann's. Daffy's, T.J. Maxx, Marshall's and Filene's Basement are also great discounters focused on sales and savings. They all have a wide selection of brands and sizes, with price points for virtually any budget. They tout major discounts compared to department store prices, up to 80% off.

I can testify that those claims are true. Clothing outlets like Nordstrom Rack, Saks Off 5th, and Neiman Marcus Last Call are similar to discounters. However, they only carry merchandise from their better known sister stores.

Manage your expectations. Discounter's merchandise is usually not damaged or irregular, but could be one or two seasons old. Therefore, it is highly unlikely that you will see the same product at Nordstrom Rack and at Nordstrom at the same time. The pickings are also slim as these discounters may only have three or four pieces of a particular style or item. Please do not get too frustrated if you cannot find your exact size, preferred design, or favorite color. Chances are that you will find something fabulous and unique regardless, as long as you can remain flexible. Some retailers, like The Gap and Ann Taylor, will develop special clothing lines that are only sold at their outlet stores. My assumption is that they can use these stores to test concepts before attempting to sell them at their larger well-established sister stores.

If you seek a very specific color, design, fit, or fabric, then do not shop at a discounter. You will leave very disappointed. However, if you are looking for a cute top to go with a pair of jeans and you are flexible, then a discounter is definitely the way to go.

FAST FASHION

Outside of discounters, *It Girls* should also consider the inexpensive fast fashion retailers like Zara, H&M, and Forever 21. They buy so much merchandise at one time, usually sourcing it from Asia, that they can transfer those discounts directly to the consumer. Another reason that their prices are so low is because they use lower quality material like acrylics and polyesters while their high-fashion designer counterparts use more costly and organic materials, like leather, silk or other expensive textiles. For this reason, some of the fabrics used by fast fashion retailers may not hold up past one season of wear, which is the downside of purchasing from some of these stores. Most *It Girls* do not mind the trade off, because it costs so little to be trend-right. These retailers are so great at keeping up with the latest trends and fresh off-the-runway fashions that some are being sued for intellectual property violations by couture designers like Diane Von Furstenberg.

Before you make a purchase at any fast fashion retailer, read all labels for the fabric information and cleaning instructions. You may be surprised by the amount of fabric care required; i.e. hand washing or dry cleaning. Also, please try on everything before you take it home. Sizing is not consistent. I know from experience that you cannot depend on the labels only to determine whether or not something will fit.

CONSIGNMENT SHOPS

Consignment shops are second-hand stores that serve as sellers of the consignor's (owner's) goods at approximately 25% of their retail value. For those *It Girls* who don't have the budget for their haute couture taste or are not willing to pay full price, a consignment shop is a great way to purchase authentic high-end merchandise, like Prada, Gucci or Chanel, on-the-cheap. Since there are laws against consigning designer knock-offs, consignment shops are obligated to authenticate all merchandise before making it available for sale.

While the merchandise is gently used, it should not be damaged. You may even find completely new merchandise. However, you should still do a thorough inspection for any damages as sales are generally final. If there is a return policy, then request a copy of it upon purchase, if it's not already on the actual receipt.

It is best to use a search engine, like google.com, to find the stores that are nearest to you as consignment shops tend to be regional and independently owned. For this reason, it is safe to assume that consignment shops in more affluent neighborhoods will have more expensive merchandise and that the converse is true in less affluent neighborhoods. Please note that there is virtually no room to haggle since the price is pre-determined between the consignor and the consignment shop (consignee) via a contractual agreement.

OFF-SEASON SHOPPING

At the end of each season, retailers will launch huge clearance sales events to make room for the next season's inventory, primarily between winter and spring, then again between summer and fall. After-Christmas sales are the best, in my opinion — especially in late January and early February when the winter merchandise starts to transition into spring. My only caution is to be patient. Since it is the end of the season, all styles and sizes will not be available. Even though you do not get that instant gratification of wearing your new garment (buying a bathing suit in the fall or winter boots in the spring), it is a great strategy for saving money.

CLEARANCE

Every *It Girl* is familiar with the incredible savings available when shopping the 'Clearance' racks. Boutiques and small stores will have one primary clearance area, which is easier to navigate. Very upscale boutiques, like Burberry, may not even have discounted merchandise in inventory. If they do have any discounts available, then the selection will not be robust. Within a larger department store, like Lord &

Taylor, you will find multiple clearance sections. Although tempting, try not to make an impulse purchase on clearance items. The ideal situation is that you find a clearance item that is very flattering to your silhouette and skin tone. Clearance racks tend to be completely unorganized, so please be patient as you dig to find your buried treasure.

LOYALTY PROGRAMS

Many retailers, including discounters, have loyalty programs. Signing up should be easy and free. With just your name and an email address, you will then be added to their distribution list for coupons and advanced notices of special sales. If you share a little more information, then you can also receive birthday-related coupons as well as other special coupons. DSW's most current program offers members a $10 coupon for every $100 spent. They keep it very simple, which is great. Don't be shy. If you do not know whether or not a retailer has a loyalty program or offers special discounts, then ask one of the sales associates, "Are there any sales going on?" or "Are there any discounts that I can take advantage of?" The average retailer covets your business and will help you to save a few dollars, if possible.

Special discounts are also made available to the credit card holders of certain retailers. Macy's is one of many department stores that has a ton of special shopping events every year that are for their credit card holders only. I do not advocate purchasing clothing on credit. You will not find a chapter in this book titled, "Charge It." However, it is only fair to mention it. If you are prudent about how you use your credit card, then you should definitely take advantage of these special savings for credit card holders.

COUPONS

For the retailer that you have particular interest in, search their site for special discounts, internet only specials, and coupons. Many retailers do offer free shipping if your purchases reach a specified spending threshold. These offers are normally not hidden because it is an incentive to purchase, so just be aware.

Couponcabin.com is also a great site that maintains a vast repository of retailer coupon codes and will even list the corresponding expiration dates. Primarily for online purchases, the benefits range from free shipping to a specific dollar amount off of a purchase to a percentage discount on a purchase.

Do not forget to pick up your Sunday and Wednesday newspapers to check out the sales circulars inside. Most national and regional department stores will leverage these circulars to promote special deals, which include coupons.

THE FITTING ROOM

How many times have you purchased clothing without trying anything on beforehand and then realized later on that a particular item did not fit? In lieu of a generous return policy, that could be the worst feeling ever. When there is no fitting room or you don't have the time to use one that is available, please understand the return policy fully before you complete your purchase. Utilizing the fitting room is not always necessary. If you are intimately involved with a particular brand or designer, in which their clothing or shoes consistently fit you like a glove, there is really no need to try anything on.

When you feel even a little uncomfortable with a garment in the fitting room — whether your bra can be seen between the shirt buttons because it's too tight, the rise in the pants is too short, or your butt does not look right in those jeans — then stop, take it off and put it back where you found it. Do not buy it. That same awkward feeling will exponentially increase when you get home and you probably won't wear it at all. If you do wear it, then you will feel very self-conscious.

To the *It Girls* out there who want to elevate your shoe game without corns or hammertoes, please try on your shoes at the store before you buy them. If your shoes feel uncomfortable when you are walking around in the store, then you better believe that they will feel 5,000 times worse when you are walking around in your daily life — at the office or outside. If you end up finding your dream pair of shoes, but your size is not available, then you may have to go up a size. There are ways to make the shoes more comfortable, including insoles, heel pads, or shoe pads for the ball of the foot. Proper support and balance are also very important, especially in the case of high heels. If you purchase shoes that are too large, then you could end up with an injury to your ankles or even your back. Shoes that are only a little tight can be stretched (assuming that they are leather) by your local shoe repair shop for a very nominal fee — probably $5 or $10 dollars.

Please do not purchase any garment, accessory or pair of shoes, unless you fall in love with it first. That's my rule. Consider tailoring only if you're in love, but the size is a little off. Keep in mind that alterations can cost more than the garment itself and may not be worth the investment. To save money, you may be tempted to use safety pins in lieu of professional tailoring. I do not recommend that approach, because they are usually not concealed well and there is a risk of injury if it one opens up unexpectedly. If you choose to use a safety pin anyway, then please hide it inconspicuously and be careful.

RETURNS

It Girls are divided on the issue of returns. Some view it as a complete hassle and a waste of time, while others consider it a normal and necessary part of the shopping process. Where do you stand?

First and foremost, *It Girls* do not purchase anything without having a complete understanding of a retailer's return policy. The risk is being stuck with unwanted merchandise. Return policies run the gamut, but they must be overtly displayed by law — on the receipt, on the hang tags, or on store signage at the cashier or near an entrance. Some retailers will do even more in order to formally alert customers about their return policy. At Forever 21, the cashiers are trained to tell every customer about the return policy before completing a sale, which includes store credit within 21 days with the receipt and hang tags attached. No cash refunds are available.

Time limits are set in all return policies, with a minimum of seven days to process a return. Some retailers allow 30 or more days. Also, you must provide a proof of purchase like a receipt. Higher end retailers will accept an attached store tag as well. Full cash refunds are not guaranteed. In certain cases, you may receive a store credit or have the ability to exchange the merchandise for something of equal value if a cash refund is not available. Clothing outlets typically do not want any merchandise returned and their policy makes that abundantly clear. You will see the following on your receipt and clearly marked on signs around the store, "ALL SALES FINAL" or "NO RETURNS/NO EXCHANGES." Other retailers have very generous return policies. At Nordstrom, I have heard that you can wear their shoes until they are worn to the ground and they will still take them back — no questions asked.

For online purchases, you will sometimes incur shipping costs to return merchandise. It is such a headache to have to go back to the post office and go through the whole process. However, you can save money on the shipping if you are able to return the merchandise directly to the store. I love Banana Republic for making that option available and I have used it — no fuss, no hassles. It is so convenient to make a return and it saves time.

Returns can be greatly minimized if you commit to only purchase merchandise you absolutely love and align with your shopping objectives. So please take a few moments to try on that accessory, garment or pair of shoes at the store prior to purchase. If you're shopping for a pair of shoes to match a handbag or a blouse to complement a specific pair of pants, then take the coordinating item with you while you shop. At a minimum, it will save you the time and energy of driving back to the store and going through the return process.

There are times when returns cannot be avoided, especially if something doesn't fit or match like you originally thought it would. Sometimes, you're just not sure or have changed your mind. At other times, *It Girls* can experience buyer's remorse. It's that overly anxious feeling you get in the pit of your stomach after purchasing something that you later regret, because you spent too much money, bought your second choice instead of your first, or succumbed to a high pressure sales associate. To reverse those negative feelings, the first step is admitting that you have made a bad decision. Then take the necessary steps to return the merchandise that you no longer need or want.

Regardless of the situation that led to your undesirable purchase, please do not discard your receipts, do not remove the tags, and do not wear the merchandise outside to avoid stains or scuffs.

POWER SHOPPING

Preparation is especially important for power shopping, which I define as shopping for three consecutive hours or more. As a former shopaholic, I have learned the importance of being physically prepared to power shop. For mothers shopping with small children, your challenges are even greater and extra preparation is required. Not only do you have to plan for the needs of your children throughout the day, but you also have to pray that they don't have a meltdown while you are shopping. I am optimistic that you can use my advice to complement or improve your current routine.

ENERGY

Make sure that you are rested and hydrated before you go shopping. I recommend that you have a good breakfast or have eaten something beforehand. Consider keeping a small bottle of water and few light snacks on hand, like a granola bar, a banana or raisins. Relatively speaking, you should feel energized throughout your shopping experience.

SHOPPING ATTIRE

If you plan to try on clothing or shoes, make sure that you can easily undress and re-dress without any fuss. My recommendation is less buttons (unless they snap), more zippers, no shoe laces, more elastic and no pullovers. It's not only about ease, but you do not want to mess up your hair or makeup either. When I'm in a serious shopping mode, I will wear a cute sweat suit with a jacket that zips, a thin tank top underneath, and flip flops.

You also have to consider factors outside of yourself — the external elements that you cannot control, like weather or air conditioning. Dress as comfortably as you can. If you're in a warmer climate, then consider breathable fabrics to minimize perspiration. Conversely, you want to dress with a few extra layers in a colder climate. When you are shopping outdoors, you may need an umbrella for rain or think about applying a strong sunscreen for extremely sunny conditions. The goal is to be completely comfortable in any environment in which you are shopping.

COMFORT

If extensive walking is involved while you shop, your handbag should be compact. Other than your wallet and a few snacks, you will want to minimize the weight on your shoulders. A five pound handbag at 9am will feel like five tons by noon. Trust me on this one! Once you add the weight of shopping bags, your arms and back will be pleading for mercy. Then your fun shopping trip will quickly turn into an unpleasant experience.

An easy solve is to invest in a light-weight, folding travel cart with wheels. You can secure your shopping bags on the cart while exponentially reducing the strain and weight on your neck, back and arms. I have even seen some people carry an empty suitcase to the mall to carry their purchases. From a security standpoint, I do not recommend that you take multiple trips to your parked vehicle to store shopping bags; especially at the mall. Your new purchases will be vulnerable to theft. It's unfortunate, but true.

TIMING

Timing is everything when you consider a shopping trip. Saturdays and Sundays are normally THE busiest shopping days of the week, because many people have time off from work. Weekends are also when most retailers compete aggressively to bring people into their stores by promoting their strongest offers and sales. For someone who does not feel like digging through racks and racks of clothing, is not interested in waiting in a long check-out line or waiting in a long line to get into the fitting room, I strongly recommend that you avoid shopping on weekends.

If you must shop on the weekend, the best time to shop is before noon. Once lunchtime hits, all bets are off. Everybody who has slept in is now up and out. During special promotional periods like Doorbusters or Early Morning Specials (think Black Friday), it will be a mob scene in the morning. Avoid, avoid, avoid — unless you have the stamina for shopping at the Olympian level.

I personally love shopping on weekdays. If you can get to a mall on Monday, Tuesday or Wednesday and there is no major holiday, you will find fewer crowds, more attentive salespeople, and less competition with other shoppers for that special item or size. You can take your time and do your thing. Actually, you will likely cover significantly more ground in less time during the weekday versus the weekend.

PARKING

Some cities have an abundance of parking, especially at the malls, while in other cities, you have to contend with very expensive parking lots or on-the-street metered parking. It's awful when you are ready to go shopping but you have to drive around for 20 minutes or more just to find a decent parking space. Either you find a parking space far from your intended destination or pay a king's ransom for a parking garage close by. Know the parking options before you venture out to avoid getting stressed. If you're not in the mood to drive or battle for a parking space, then try public transportation.

CASH

At a flea market or street fair, most purchases are a cash-n-carry situation. If you do not have enough cash on you, then you will have to use a local ATM and probably incur some ridiculous fees. Many of these vendors are armed with the latest technology to accept credit cards for purchases, but they incur a fee for each credit card transaction processed. From a haggling standpoint, they will be much more flexible in negotiating a price if you are paying for the entire purchase in cash. Another thing to consider is identity theft. Unfortunately, you really have no point of reference for these merchants that travel from street fair to street fair. Some are not ethical. To mitigate those issues, cash is a good solve. You will have to gage the amount of cash to keep on hand depending on the type of purchase you plan to make. Each individual's situation is unique, so you will have to judge what works best for you.

THE IT GIRL RULES REWOUND

1. *Love the body that you have today — knowing that it is beautiful and unique.*

2. *Fit accounts for over 50% of the success of any look.*

3. *Panty lines should never be seen through pants, dresses, skirts, shorts, or jeans — ever, ever, never, never!*

4. *When you check out your outfit in the mirror, do not only look at the front. Use a second mirror and look at the back too.*

5. *Ask for referrals before choosing a tailor.*

6. *Colors are fun. Embrace them.*

7. *Dry cleaning is best for hand washable garments.*

8. *Always ask for a black cloth napkin when dining at a restaurant to avoid lint.*

9. *Whatever style statement you choose, put your personal signature on it.*

10. *Fake it until you make it.*

11. *Fierce designs with understated labels and logos are ideal.*

12. *Audit your closet first before you start shopping.*

13. *To curtail closet clutter, replace or discard something old each time you purchase something new.*

14. *You do not have to pay full price for amazing clothing, accessories, shoes, or even makeup, unless you want to.*

15. *Do not purchase anything without having a complete understanding of a retailer's return policy.*

16. *Do not purchase any garment, accessory or pair of shoes, unless you fall in love with it first.*

AUTHOR'S NOTE

The brands, companies and/or products described in The It Girl Rules in no way endorse or sponsor this book. The author mentions these brands, companies, and products to better guide her readers and will not be compensated for any reference.

Made in the USA
Monee, IL
17 February 2023